Brianna

My Tall Book of Psalms

Poems by
Donna Huisjen

Pictures by
Cindy Salans Rosenheim

Zonder**kidz**
The Children's Group of ZondervanPublishingHouse

To Amanda, Angela, and Khristina,
with love from Mom
For the Lord is good and his love endures forever;
his faithfulness continues through all generations
—Psalm 100:5
D.H.

This collection of illustrations is dedicated to Nicky,
who brought them to life.
C.S.R.

My Tall Book of Psalms: Favorite Psalms in Rhyme
Text copyright © 1999 by Donna Huisjen
Illustrations copyright © 1999 by the Zondervan Corporation
ISBN 0-310-918618

Requests for information should be addressed to:

ZondervanPublishingHouse
Mail Drop B20
Grand Rapids, Michigan 49530
http://www.zondervan.com

Library of Congress Catalog Card Number 98–61558

This edition printed on acid-free paper and meets the American National Standards Institute Z39.48 standard.

Illustrations by Cindy Salans Rosenheim

Printed in China

99 00 01 02 03/HK/ 10 9 8 7 6 5 4 3 2 1

This book belongs

to

Derrik Butler

The Book of Psalms

The Bible is not just one book.
Inside its covers hide
a tall, tall stack of books, for it
holds sixty-six inside!

God's Spirit gave his words to men.
They wrote what they were told.
The psalms are poems of praise to God.
These poems are very old!

King David wrote down many psalms.
He loved to dance and sing.
When he was just a boy he killed
Goliath with his sling!

How to find the psalms within
God's Word is not a riddle.
To find this book is easy—
it's exactly in the middle!

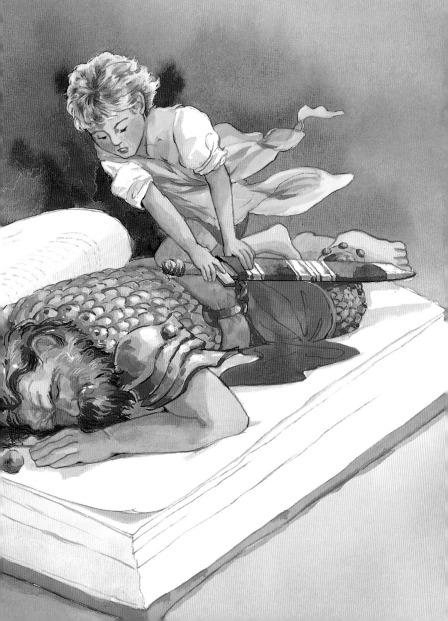

Psalm 2:1–4

O God, you are King over all of the earth,
over crickets and rocket ships, anthills and art,
the Creator of planets and pandas and pears.
You are King of all nations—and King of my heart.

Then why, God, do bad kings think they are
   so strong?
Why do they think they can make all the rules?
They think they are smarter and better than you.
They think they're so smart—but you say
   they are fools!

I'd laugh if my puppy thought he was my boss
or if I imagined a tiger I drew
pounced right off the page, shook his great paw
   at me,
and thought he could tell me what I had to do.

Your Word says you sit up in heaven and laugh
when people you've made think they're smarter
   than you.
I think that they know, God, that you are in charge.
They know but don't want to believe that it's true!

Psalm 5:1–3,7–8,11–12

When I open my eyes in the morning,
I stretch both my legs and my arms.
Then I shut my eyes tight one more minute,
and I pray that you'll keep me from harm.

For I know that my day will be busy.
There are lots of things I want to do.
But whatever might happen today, God,
I expect that you'll help me get through.

In my heart I bow down toward your temple,
and I climb up your holy hill.
Lord, I pray that I'll march on a straight path
with no detours away from your will.

Please protect me this day, God, and give me
a day full of gifts from above.
Even after my feet touch the cold floor,
wrap me up in your blanket of love.

Psalm 6:1–4,6–10

Today I did a wrong thing—
no one else knows what I did.
I took my best friend's favorite toy,
then sneaked away and hid.

O please, God, don't be angry.
I have to let you know
I'm crying deep inside,
but I'm afraid to let it show.

I'll pray, "God, please forgive me!"
Then I'll go and find my friend.
I'll say "I'm sorry," give it back—
we'll be best friends again.

Sometimes I let the devil find
a way inside my heart.
But when I ask, you kick him out—
I get a brand new start!

Psalm 7:3–5,8–9,15–17

"You cannot hide from God," Mom said.
"You're always in his sight."
So I can't sneak away from you,
not even when it's night!

Your eyes are always on me, God,
and anytime I sin,
it's like I dig a great big hole
and then I fall right in.

For sin is like a boomerang
I throw with all my might,
but every time it flies right back
in one big round-trip flight!

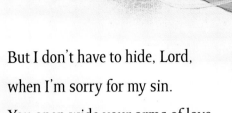

But I don't have to hide, Lord,
when I'm sorry for my sin.
You open wide your arms of love
and call me to hop in!

Psalm 8

Your name, O Lord, is wonderful.
I lift my hands in praise.
Your glory's high and all around,
like clouds or sunshine rays.

O God, I like to finger paint
and make clay horses too.
But I can't paint a sunset or
shape elephants like you.

Creation tells how great you are,
but I'm so very small.
I worry I'm too little, God,
for you to love at all.

But even babies sing to you
as they begin to grow.
You say that kids are special,
and you love me—this I know!

Psalm 19:1-4

I'd like to tell the whole world, God,
about your love and care,
but I just know one language,
so I can't talk everywhere!

I'm getting good at English,
but I don't know Taiwanese
or German, Cree or Hutu,
and I can't speak Portuguese.

But, God, there is one language
that all people understand.
They see the beauty you've created
with your skillful hands.

The stallion neighs; the donkey brays;
the wolf howls wild and free.
The sunrise and the waterfall
shout, "Look, for God made me!"

Psalm 23

I am your lamb, and you're my good Shepherd—
you give me each day what is best.
I can lie on a blanket of grass by the stream,
and you'll sit by my side while I rest.

I am your sheep, and you're my kind Shepherd—
you care for me all day and night.
When I walk in the dark, and the shadows creep close,
you will not let me out of your sight.

You sprinkle cool raindrops of blessings on me—
you make my small cup overflow.
I skitter and skip like a curious lamb,
for your love goes wherever I go.

I am your sheep, God—you watch over me,
and you give me each day all I need.
Your goodness will follow wherever I roam—
so I'll follow wherever you lead!

Psalm 27:1,5,11,14

Your Word is like a lantern, Lord,
that lights the woods at night.
You hold my hand in yours,
so I am sure I'll be all right.

I'm not afraid of creatures, God,
that hoot or growl or crawl.
I'm not afraid that holes or sticks
might make me trip and fall.

You pick me up and set me
on a rock, secure and dry.
No slimy thing can touch my toes
when I am way up high.

I'm certain you will guide my feet
along the path—I know
that I won't walk in circles
for you'll show me where to go.

Psalm 29:1–5,7,10–11

I praise you for your glory, God.
I play my drum and sing,
for you are great and good,
and you deserve the praise I bring.

But, Lord, I'm scared of angry waves
that rear and roar at sea,
or thunder when it cracks its whip
of lightning close to me.

You care about a child like me.
You see me when it storms.
And even when the power goes out,
we burrow, dry and warm.

For you're in charge of snow and rain,
of lightning, wind and wave.
You wrap me safely in your peace,
and then I'm calm and brave.

Psalm 30

I'll praise you, God. When I am sad
and no one else is near,
you pick me up and hug me close
and wipe away each tear.

I know your love, Lord, s-t-r-e-t-c-h-e-s long,
just like a rubber band,
from night to day, from months to years—
too long to understand!

Some days I wake up feeling strong,
like I could run a mile.
But then the clouds hold up their hands
to hide the sun's bright smile.

Then, God, I call to you for help.
The sunlight wriggles in
and with warm sunbeams tickles me
right underneath my chin!

Psalm 33:1–3,6–7,10–11,13–22

Sing with joy to the Lord, all you children.
It is right to sing praise to our King—
to praise him with dancing, recorder or flute
or an old-fashioned lyre with ten strings.

You created the world just by speaking, O Lord.
Your breath formed each planet and star.
You gathered the sea water with your own hands
the way I catch rain in a jar.

The nations plan wars to gain power,
but the ending is not in their hands,
for you are in charge; you control everything,
and all history follows your plans.

No nation is saved by brave soldiers
or by sneaky Stealth bombers or tanks.
But your sleepless eyes watch the children you love.
You protect us—so let us give thanks!

Psalm 34:1–7,11

I'll praise you, God—I'll shout and tell
all children of your care.
Come, boys and girls, join in my song—
sing here and everywhere!

I prayed to you when I was scared
of noises in the night.
I asked for help; you told me,
"Everything will be all right!"

I prayed, God, when I felt ashamed.
My cheeks were hot and red.
You turned my frown face down-side-up
and made me smile instead.

When it is dark, your angel camps
right on my bedroom floor.
We whisper and we giggle—
I'm not lonely anymore!

Psalm 36:5,7–8,10

Your love, O God, is everywhere—
it fills the sky and seas.
It's cradled deep inside my heart—
it whispers in the trees.

No money, God, could buy your love,
but that's okay—it's free!
It's better than a pot of gold,
and it's your gift to me!

Your love is free for rich or poor.
Strong men and children too
can nestle in the shadow
of your wings and rest in you.

Your love can never run out, God—
I'm really not sure why.
You pour your love and pour some more—
your bucket's never dry!

Psalm 42:1-2,7,11

Like a deer pants for cold, rushing water
or a runner puffs after a race,
so my spirit is thirsty for you, Lord,
for a drink of your love and your grace.

I remember one time I was playing
with my giant, red ball at the beach.
I got dunked and rolled 'round by a big wave
so the fresh air was out of my reach.

I was scared! I choked and I sputtered!
And my lungs felt just like they'd burst.
My friends saw me go under and ran, Lord,
but my dad's strong arms picked me up first.

Sometimes life brings me danger and trouble,
but you're there, God, and you understand.
When I'm thirsty you give me cool water.
If I'm drowning you'll hold out your hand!

Psalm 46:1–2,10–11

I like to make a fist and feel
my muscle; Lord, someday
I hope that I'll be strong and tough,
but you're my strength today!

For even if the ground caved in
or if a mountain tall
would tumble to the ocean floor,
you'd hear my frightened call!

You're with me everywhere;
no matter where I am, you're near.
You're never absent, God; I call
your name—you say, "I'm here!

"Ssshhhssshhh!!! Listen! Just be quiet,
stop one moment and stand still.
Remember you're my child.
I love you, and I always will!"

Psalm 55:6,8,16,22

Sometimes I wish I had a pair
of wings, just like a dove.
I'd flap those wings and look way down
at earth from high above.

In times of trouble I could spread
my wings to fly away.
I'd build a cozy nest where I'd
be safe both night and day.

I'd find a special place where
I'd stay dry through every storm.
Beneath a big rock on a cliff
I'd curl up, sleepy-warm.

The wind could moan outside my nest,
but God would hear me call.
I wouldn't have to worry
on that cliff—birds never fall!

Psalm 56:1,3–4,11,13

O God, I'm scared of lots of things:
my closet when it's dark,
imaginary monsters, snakes,
fierce dogs that snarl and bark.

I'm scared of people sometimes too.
I just can't trust them all.
I worry I'll get kidnapped.
(What if no one hears me call?)

Your Word, though, says I can relax.
You're with me constantly.
Because you see all things, O God,
what harm can people do to me?

You keep my feet from stumbling
in the dark; you guide my shoes.
Your Word shines like a flashlight
on the path that leads to you.

Psalm 69:1–3,13–17

My day has been all wrong, Lord.
It was bad right from the first.
But then it went from bad to worse
and then from worse to *worst*.

I've been in trouble several times;
I just can't seem to win.
I feel as though I'm stuck in quicksand—
sunk up to my chin!

I'm all worn out from crying;
my throat is dry and sore.
My eyes are red and puffy;
I can't take any more!

I thank you for you heard me cry,
and now I want to say,
"I'm sorry, God; please make
tomorrow be a better day!"

Psalm 73:2–4,8,12–13,18,23

I tried ice skating yesterday morning.
My legs wouldn't obey me at all.
Each one skated a different direction;
then the rest of me just had to fall!

Lord, my neighbor was there—he's a bully.
He is tall, and his muscles are strong.
When I'd fall, he'd skate circles around me;
then he'd laugh—I think that was wrong!

I try hard to love and obey you,
but my neighbor boy just doesn't care.
I wonder what good that it does me
to do right—God, it just isn't fair!

Your Word says the wicked will someday
have their turn, Lord, to stumble and fall.
But your strong hand will hold my
    hand tightly;
then the ice won't seem slippery at all!

Psalm 81:1–2,6–7,10,16

I shout with joy to you, O God;
I dance and clap and sing.
With tambourine and rhythm sticks
I praise your name, my King.

For you've forgiven me—my sins
were like a heavy pack
of books I had to carry,
but you took them off my back!

I feed my baby sister
and I tell her, "Open wide!"
And when I open up my heart,
you pour your love inside!

You hold your hand out to me—
filled with good things from above.
You fill me with my favorite foods
and feed my soul with love.

Psalm 84:1–3,10–12

Your church, God, is a special place;
I love to visit there,
to praise you in your own house
though I know you're everywhere!

One day with you is better, Lord,
than thousands on my own.
You are my sunshine and my shield;
I can't survive alone.

A bird, God, makes her cozy nest
beneath your watchful eye.
You keep her babies safe and warm
until they learn to fly.

I'm like a little bird because
your eye is on me too!
Just when I need your help the most,
a blessing comes from you.

Psalm 96:1,11–13

Today I learned a brand new song,
O Lord, of praise to you.
And all creation sings with me,
the streams and songbirds too!

All nature joins the happy tune
with clucking, b-a-a-a or moo,
with ribbet, squawk or squeak or neigh
or cock–a–doodle–doo.

Hyena, add your tee–hee–hee,
woodpecker, rat–tat–tat.
Barn owl, join in with hoo–hoo–hoo
and rain with pitter–pat.

Old oak tree, raise your leafy arms
and clap to God your Maker,
then sway your heavy trunk and dance
in praise to your Creator!

Psalm 100

Shout with gladness to God, all you children.
Come to him with your present of song.
Wrap your love up in praise like a package
with a ribbon and bring it along.

You are his, because he's your Creator.
He's with you—you're never alone!
He is yours—he's the Father who loves you.
He's your owner, but still he's your own.

So come into his house with thanksgiving.
Gladly enter his gates singing praise.
Give your very best gifts to your Maker
for the gift of his love all your days.

He was God to your grandmas and grandpas.
Your great–grandmas and great–grandpas
    knew
the kind care of the same heavenly Father
who will love your great–grandchildren too!

Psalm 103:1,11–12,15–17

I want to praise your name, O God,
with heart and voice to sing,
with waving arms and tapping toes
to dance for you, my King.

Your love is high and wide and deep,
O Lord, but what is best:
You throw my sins as far away
as east is from the west.

All people are like wildflowers,
with bright colors—everywhere!
A strong wind blows; they fly away;
there's no sign that they were there!

But you do not forget your children
when they've blown away.
They're your bouquet in heaven;
they'll be with you every day!

Psalm 104:1–3,10–13,27–28,33–34

O God, you are so great.
You made all things; you're everywhere.
You ride the wind; you wear the light;
you're in the sea and air.

You stretch the sky above us like
a great big circus tent.
You squeeze the clouds just like a sponge;
your rain is heaven-sent!

All creatures look to you for food;
you open up your hand.
They fly and swim and run to you
from sky and sea and land.

You care for all of my needs too—
good food, warm hugs, best friends,
clean air, a family all my own—
your love, Lord, never ends.

Psalm 121

I throw my head back, God, and look
straight up, right at the sky.
I know you're looking back at me
from heaven way up high.

You stay awake all night and keep
me safe from head to toes.
And I can shut my eyes because
your eyes will never close.

At noontime when the sun is hot,
you're like a shady tree.
But when the sun slides down, God,
you're a kind, warm friend to me.

You watch me every minute,
when I work or when I play.
You're with me when I stay at home
and when I go away.

Psalm 127:2

"You shouldn't burn the candle
at both ends," I heard Dad say.
I laughed—I didn't think that I
could do it anyway!

He told me that some grown-ups want
to give the Lord their best.
And so they work long hours each day—
they hardly ever rest!

They start at dawn and quit long after
dusk turns into night.
It's dark at both ends of the day—
they need a lamp for light.

We use electric lights; we don't
need candles anymore.
But Dad says nighttime is God's gift
and sleeping's what it's for!

Psalm 139:1–3,13–18

O God, you know me upside down,
up straight and inside out.
You know my wishes, hopes and dreams,
my thoughts and fears and doubts.

You see me when I'm here or there
or when I stand or sit
or stretch or wiggle, skip or hop,
or tickle, kick or hit.

Before the day that I was born
your hands were forming me.
You knew what I would look like, God—
you knew just who I'd be!

To count your blessings is like counting
beach sand by the sea.
I fall asleep while counting—
when I wake, you're still with me.

Psalm 147:16–18

Sometimes, O God, in winter
I imagine I can see
that you're in heaven working on
a giant recipe.

You sift the fluffy snow,
then add a dash of sugar-sleet.
You throw in yellow daffodils
and bright green winter wheat.

You mix it with the whirling wind,
and set it in the sun.
You'll drizzle frosting later with
some sprinkles when it's done.

The warm sun is your oven, God—
it melts the wintry blast.
You stir warm breezes with your spoon,
and springtime comes at last!

My Tall Book of Psalms
Favorite Psalms in Rhyme

Donna Huisjen *lives in Grand Rapids, MI, and is the single adoptive parent of three daughters, ages 13, 17, and 21. A graduate of Calvin College in Grand Rapids, Ms. Huisjen is an editorial assistant at Zondervan Publishing House.*

Cindy Salans Rosenheim *is a graduate of Tufts University in Medford, MA. Ms. Rosenheim has been an illustrator for more than twenty years, specializing in children's illustration and design. She lives with her husband and their three sons in San Francisco, CA.*

Editorial by **Ruth A. DeJager**
Art Direction & Design by **Jody Langley**